# Swallows

Written by Sandra Iversen

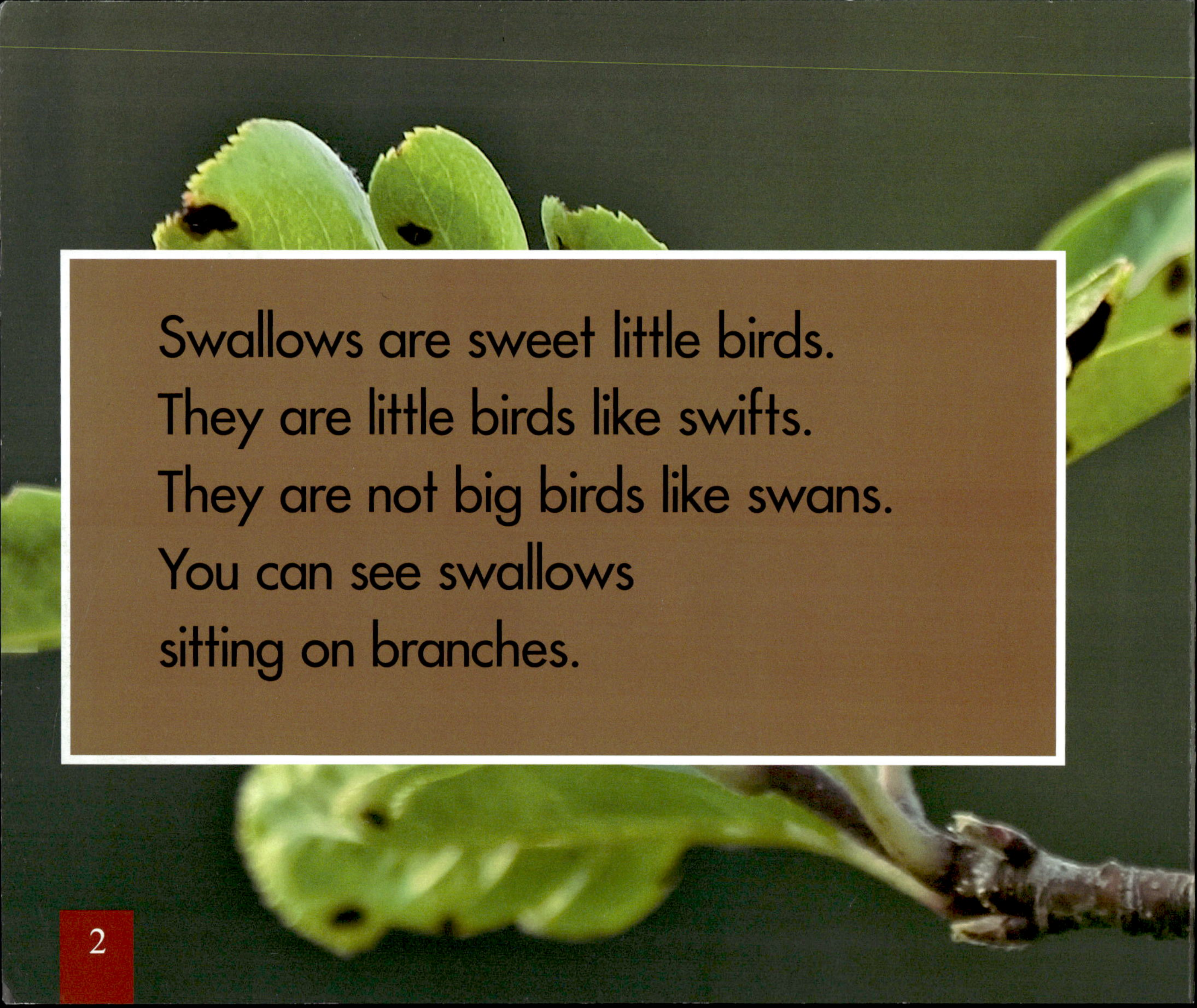

Swallows are sweet little birds.
They are little birds like swifts.
They are not big birds like swans.
You can see swallows
sitting on branches.

swallow
branch

This swallow sits on a wire.
Look at its long wings.
Look at its long tail.

This one sits by its nest.
Look at its white chest.
Look at its blue feathers.
Look at its red face.

Swallows make nests
to lay their eggs.
They make nests up high.
They make them of mud and grass.
This one is on some bricks.

This one is on some wood.

Swallows feed their babies.
This one feeds its babies in the nest.

This baby sits on a wire to get fed.

When it gets cold,
swallows fly to a hot place.

# Where Swallows Fly in Winter

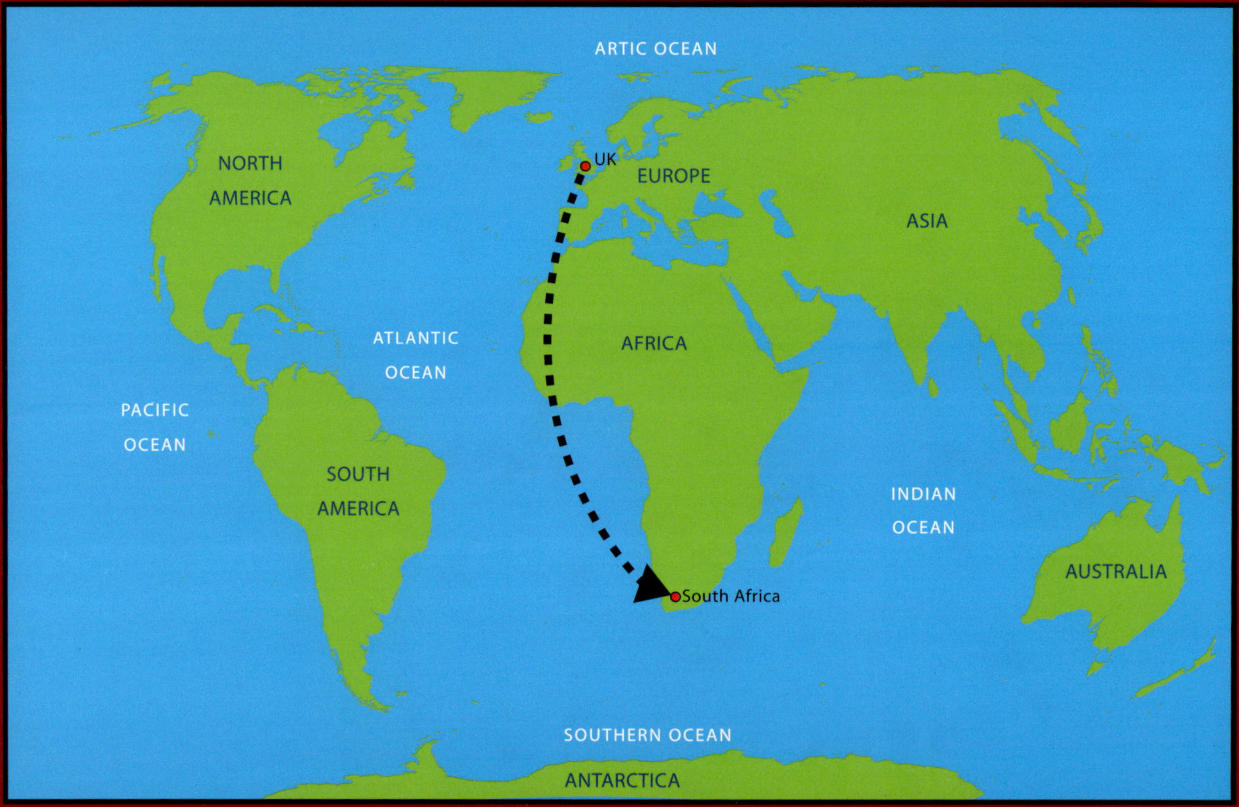